Icelandic 101: A Practical Guide for Beginners

Icelandic 101: A Practical Guide for Beginners

By: Project Fluency

Table of Contents

Please Note

This is a book summary. Copyright © 2016 by Project Fluency. All rights reserved worldwide. No part of this publication may be reproduced or transmitted in any form without the prior written consent of the publisher. Limit of Liability/Disclaimer of Warranty: The publisher and author make no representations or warranties with respect to the accuracy or completeness of these contents and disclaim all warranties such as warranties of fitness for a particular purpose. The author or publisher is not liable for any damages whatsoever. The fact that an individual or organization is referred to in this document as a citation or source of information does not imply that the author or publisher endorses the information that the individual or organization provided.

Icelandic 101: A Practical Guide for Beginners

Table of Contents

Pronunciation 7
- Vowels 8
- Consonants 10
- Diphthongs 13

Phrases and Vocabulary 15
- Basics 16
- Problems 21
- Numbers 23
- Time 34
- Colors 41
- Transportation 43
- Lodging 51
- Money 54
- Eating 56
- Bars 62
- Shopping 65
- Driving 69
- Authority 71

Bonus Icelandic Slang 73

Pronunciation

Icelandic 101: A Practical Guide for Beginners

Vowels

A a

(Short) like "a" in "land", (long) like "a" in "car"; or like "ow" in "now" when followed by "ng" or "nk".

Á á

Like "ow" in "now".

E e

(Short) like "e" in "met", (long) like "ea" in "bear".

É é

Like "ye" in "yes".

I i

(Short) like "i" in "bit", (long) same "i" but lengthened; or like "ee" in "meet" when followed by "ng" or "nk".

Í í

Like "ee" in "meet".

O o

(Short) like "o" in "hot", (long) like "or" in "door".

Ó ó

Like "o" in "snow".

U u

(Short) like "u" in "put", (long) the same short "u" but lengthened; or like "oo" in "moon" when followed by "ng" or "nk".

Ú ú

Like "oo" in "moon".

Y y

Same as Icelandic "i": (short) like "i" in "bit", (long) same "i" but lengthened; or like "ee" in "meet" when followed by "ng" or "nk".

Ý ý

Same as Icelandic "í": like "ee" in "meet".

Æ æ

Like "i" in "mile".

Ö ö

(Short) like "ur" in "fur" but shorter, (long) like "ur" in "fur"; (**do not** pronouce the "r").

Icelandic 101: A Practical Guide for Beginners

Consonants

B b

    Like "b" in "bed", or like "p" when at word end or following "m".

D d

    Like "d" in "day", or like "t" when at word end.

Ð ð

    Like "th" in "that", (only occurs in word middle and word end).

F f

    Like "f" in "fish", or like "v" in "van" when between vowels; or when before "l" or "n", like "b" in "bed".

G g

    Like "g" in "go", or like "k" in "kill" when in word middle; it is lost after "á", "ó", "u" when followed by "a" or "u" in the next syllable or when at word end.

H h

    Like "h" in "hat", or like "k" when before a consonant; (never silent like "honour").

J j

Like "y" in "yes".

K k

Like "k" in "kill".

L l

Like "l" in "like".

M m

Like "m" in "me".

N n

Like "n" in "nurse".

P p

Like "p" in "push", or like "f" in "far" when before "s", "k", or "t".

R r

Rolled, like Scottish "r".

S s

Like "s" in "sun"; (never like "z" in "zero").

T t

Like "t" in "take".

V v

Icelandic 101: A Practical Guide for Beginners

    Like "v" in "value".

X x

    Like "x" in "exit".

Þ þ

    Like "th" in "thing".

Diphthongs

au

> Like "ur" in "fur" (do not pronounce the r) followed by "ee" in "see" but with no intervening "r" - "u(r)-ee", similar to "oy" in "boy".

ei, ey

> Like "ay" in "say".

gi, gj

> Like "gy" in "drag-you" at word start; like "y" in "yes" in word middle or at word end.

hv

> Like "kv" in "lock vent".

kk

> Like "chk" in Scottish "Loch Carron".

ll

> Like "tl" in "settle". Similar to Welsh "ll" (double L) but more aspirated (has more air to it).

ng

> Like "nk" in "thinker", not "ng" in "finger".

nn

Like "dn" in "hard-nosed" when after "á", "é", "í", "ó", "ú", "ý", "æ", "au", "ei", or "ey"; or like "nn" in "tunnel" after "a", "e", "i", "o", "u", "y" or "ö".

pp

Like "h" and "p" fused together, similar to "hop" without the "o".

rl

Like "dl" in "riddle" similar in form to Welsh "ll" (double L) but said harder.

rn

Like "dn" in "hard-nosed" when after "á", "é", "í", "ó", "ú", "ý", "æ", "au", "ei", or "ey".

tt

Like "h" and "t" fused together, similar to "hut" without the "u".

Phrases and Vocabulary

Basics

Hello.

    Halló. (*Hal-law*)

Hello (informal).

    Sæll, (to a man). *(Sight-l.)*

    Sæl, (to a woman). *(Sigh-l.)*

Hi.

    Hæ. *(High.) Like the English word. Common amongst younger generations.*

How are you?

    Hvað segirðu gott? *(Kvadh sek-ir-dhu goht?)*

Fine, thank you.

    Ég segi allt gott, þakka þér fyrir. *(Yeh sek-i atlt goht, thah-ka thyer fi-rir.)*

What is your name?

    Hvað heitirðu? *(Kvadh hay-tir-dhu?)*

My name is _____ .

    Ég heiti _____ . *(Yeh hay-ti _____ .)*

Nice to meet you.

Komdu sæll, (to a man). *(Komdu sight-l.)*

Komdu sæl, (to a woman). *(Komdu sighl.)*

Please.

Gjörðu svo vel, (to one person). *(Gyer-dhu svo vel.)*

Or; Gerið þið svo vel, (to many people). *(Ger-adh thi-dh svo vel.)*

Thank you.

Þakka þér fyrir. *(Thah-ka thyer fi-rir.)*

Thanks, (informal)

Takk. *(Tahk.)*

You're welcome.

Ekkert að þakka. *(Eh-kehrt adh thah-ka.)*

Yes.

Já. *(Yaw.)*

Or; Jú *(Yoo; for answering a negative question).*

No.

Nei. *(Nay.)*

Excuse me, (getting attention).

Afsakið. *(Av-sak-idh.)*

Excuse me, (begging pardon).

Icelandic 101: A Practical Guide for Beginners

    Fyrirgefðu. *(Fi-rir-gyev-dhu.)*

I'm sorry, (didn't hear).

    Ha? *(Ha?)*

    Or; Hvað segir þú? *(Kvadh se-kir thoo?)*

I'm sorry, (regretful).

    Því miður. *(Thvee mi-dhur.)*

Goodbye

    Faravel. *(Fa-ra-vel; this is **very** formal and should only be used with complete strangers.)*

Goodbye, (informal).

    Bless. *(Bless; often said twice, "Bless bless".)*

I can't speak Icelandic [well].

    Ég tala ekki íslensku [svo vel]. *(Yeh ta-la eh-ki ees-len-sku [svo vel].)*

Do you speak English?

    Talarðu ensku? *(Ta-lar-dhu en-sku?)*

Is there someone here who speaks English?

    Er einhver hér sem talar ensku? *(Er ayn-kver hyer sem ta-lar en-sku?)*

Help!

    Hjálp! *(Hyawlp!)*

Phrases & Vocabulary

Look out!

    Gætinn! *(Gigh-tin!)*

Good morning.

    Góðan daginn. *(Goh-dhan da-kin.)*

Good evening.

    Gott kvöld. *(Got kvur-lt.)*

Good night.

    Góða nótt. *(Goh-dha no-ht.)*

Good night, (to sleep).

    Sofðu vel. *(So-vdhu vel.)*

I don't understand.

    Ég skil ekki. *(Yeh skil eh-ki.)*

Could you speak more slowly?

    Gætirðu talað hægar? *(Gigh-tir-dhu ta-ladh high-kar?)*

How do you say _____ in Icelandic?

    Hvernig segir maður _____ á íslensku?
    (Kver-nik se-kir ma-dhur _____ aw ees-len-sku?)

OK.

Icelandic 101: A Practical Guide for Beginners

Allt í lagí. *(Atlt ee lak-i.)*

Or; Ókei *(Oh-kay; this is used amongst younger generations.)*

Where is the toilet?

Hvar er klósettið? *(Kvar er klow-sett-idh?)*

Problems

Leave me alone.

    Farðu í burtu. Or just "farðu" *(Fa-r thu i bur-tu.)*

Don't touch me!

    Ekki snerta mig! *(E-kki snert-a mig.)*

I'll call the police.

    Ég kalla á lögreglunna. *(Ye kat-la a lurk-rek-luna.)*

Police!

    Lögregla! *(Lurk-rek-la!)*

Stop! Thief!

    Stopp! Þjófur! *(Sto-hp! Thyoh-vur!)*

I need your help.

    Ég þarf smá hjálp. *(Ye tharf sm-a hjowlp.)*

It's an emergency.

    Það er áríðandi. *(Thadh er awr-eedh-an-ti.)*

I'm lost.

    Ég er týndur. *(Yeg er teen-tur.)*

My bag is missing.

    Taskan mín er týnd. *(Tas-kan meen er teen-ed.)*

Icelandic 101: A Practical Guide for Beginners

My wallet is missing.

>Leðurveskið mitt er týnt. *(Ledh-ur-ves-kidh mi-ht er teent.)*

My purse is missing.

>Buddan mín er týnd. *(Bu-tan meen er teen-ed.)*

I'm sick.

>Ég er veikur. *(Yeg er vai-kur.)*

I've been injured.

>Ég er særður. *(Yeg er sair-thur.)*

I need a doctor.

>Ég þarf lækni. *(Yeg tha-rf lai-kni.)*

Can I use your phone?

>Má ég nota símann þinn? *(Maw ye not-a see-min thin?)*

Numbers

number _____ (train, bus, etc.)

    númer _____ *(noo-mer)*

half

    hálfur *(hawl-vur)*

third

    þriðji *(thri-dhyi)*

quarter

    fjórðungur *(fjohr-dhun-gur)*

less

    minni *(min-ni)*

more

    meiri *(may-ri)*

Icelandic 101: A Practical Guide for Beginners

Cardinal

Examples:

(m) *Einn maður (ay-tn madh-ur)* "one man".

(f) *Ein kona (ayn kon-a)* "one woman".

(n) *Eitt barn (ay-ht barn)* "one child".

1

einn, (masculine) *(a-te) much like the word "eight or ate" but with a softer T*

ein, (feminine) *(ayn)*

eitt, (neuter) *(ay-ht)*

2

tveir, (masculine) *(tvay-r)*

tvær, (feminine) *(tvigh-r)*

tvö, (neuter) *(two-ah) much like the word "Twas" without the S*

3

þrír, (masculine) *(threer)*

þrjár, (feminine) *(three-aw)*

þrjú, (neuter) *(three-oo)*

4

fjórir, (masculine) *(fjoh-rir)*

fjórar, (feminine) *(fjoh-rar)*

Phrases & Vocabulary

fjögur, (neuter) *(fyoh-ur)*

5

fimm *(fim)*

6

sex *(sex)*

7

sjö *(syur)*

8

átta *(ohw-ta)*

9

níu *(nee-u)*

10

tíu *(tee-u)*

11

ellefu *(et-le-vu)*

12

tólf *(toe-lv)*

13

Icelandic 101: A Practical Guide for Beginners

þrettán *(threh-tawn)*

14

fjórtán *(fyohr-tawn)*

15

fimmtán *(fim-tawn)*

16

sextán *(sex-tawn)*

17

sautján *(sur-ee-tyawn)*
Or, seytján *(say-tjawn)*

18

átján *(aw-tyawn)*

19

nítján *(nee-tyawn)*

20

tuttugu *(tuh-tu-ghu)*

21

tuttugu og einn *(tuh-tu-ghu oh aydn)*

Phrases & Vocabulary

22

    tuttugu og tveir *(tuh-tu-ghu oh tvayr)*

23

    tuttugu og þrír *(tuh-tu-ghu oh threer)*

30

    þrjátíu *(thryaw-tee-u)*

40

    fjörutíu *(fyoh-ru-tee-u)*

50

    fimmtíu *(fim-tee-u)*

60

    sextíu *(sex-tee-u)*

70

    sjötíu *(syur-tee-u)*

80

    áttatíu *(awh-ta-tee-u)*

90

    níutíu *(nee-u-tee-u)*

100

Icelandic 101: A Practical Guide for Beginners

    hundrað *(hun-tradh)*

101

    hundrað og einn *(hun-tradh oh ay-dn)*

200

    tvö hundruð *(tvur hun-trudh)*

300

    þrjú hundruð *(thryow hun-trudh)*

1000

    þúsund *(thoo-sunt)*

2000

    tvö þúsund *(tvur thoo-sunt)*

100,000

    hundrað þúsund *(hun-tradh thoo-sunt)*

1,000,000

    milljón *(mil-yohn)*

1,000,000,000

    miljarður *(mil-yar-dhur)*

1,000,000,000

    billjón *(bil-yohn)*

Ordinal

1st

    fyrsti *(fir-sti)*

2nd

    annar *(an-nar)*

3rd

    þriðji *(thri-dhyi)*

4th

    fjórði *(fyohr-dhi)*

5th

    fimmti *(fim-ti)*

6th

    sjötti *(syur-ti)*

7th

    sjöundi *(syur-unti)*

8th

    áttundi *(awt-unti)*

9th

Icelandic 101: A Practical Guide for Beginners

níundi *(nee-unti)*

10th

tíundi *(tee-unti)*

11th

ellefti *(et-lev-ti)*

12th

tólfti *(tohlv-ti)*

13th

þrettándi *(thre-ht-awn-ti)*

14th

fjórtándi *(fyohr-tawn-ti)*

15th

fimmtándi *(fim-tawn-ti)*

16th

sextándi *(sex-tawn-ti)*

17th

sautjándi *(sur-eet-yawn-ti)*
Or, seytjándi *(say-tyawn-ti)*

18th

    átjándi *(awt-yawn-ti)*

19th

    nítjándi *(neet-yawn-ti)*

20th

    tuttugasti *(tut-htu-kas-ti)*

21st

    tuttugasti og fyrsti *(tut-htu-kas-ti oh fir-sti)*

30th

    þrítugasti *(three-tu-kas-ti)*

40th

    fertugasti *(fer-tu-kas-ti)*

50th

    fimmtugasti *(fim-tu-kas-ti)*

60th

    sextugasti *(sex-tu-kas-ti)*

70th

    sjötugasti *(syur-tu-kas-ti)*

Icelandic 101: A Practical Guide for Beginners

80th

    áttugasti *(awt-tu-kas-ti)*

90th

    nítugasti *(nee-tu-kas-ti)*

100th

    hundraðasti *(hun-tra-dhas-ti)*

101st

    hundraðasti og fyrsti *(hun-tra-dhas-ti oh fir-sti)*

100th

    tvöhundruðasti *(tvur-hun-tra-dhas-ti)*

1,000th

    þúsundasti *(thoo-sun-tas-ti)*

2,000th

    tvöþúsundasti *(tur-thoo-sun-tas-ti)*

100,000th

    hundrað þúsuntasti *(hun-tradh thoo-sun-tas-ti)*

1,000,000th

    milljónasti *(mil-yohn-asti)*

1,000,000,000th

þúsund milljónasti *(thoo-sunt mil-yohn-asti)*

1,000,000,000,000th

billjónasti *(bil-yohn-asti)*

Icelandic 101: A Practical Guide for Beginners

Time

now
    núna *(noo-na)y*

early
    snemma *(sne-ma)*

late
    seint *(saynt)*

before
    áður en *(awdh-ur en)*

later
    seinna meir *(say-na may-r)*

morning
    morgunn *(mor-kun)*

afternoon
    eftirmiðdagur *(eb-tir-midh-tak-ur)*

evening
    kvöld *(kvurlt)*

night
    nótt *(no-ht)*

Clock Time

one o'clock AM

> klukkan er eitt *(kluch-kan er ay-ht)*

two o'clock AM

> klukkan er tvö *(kluck-kan er tvur)*

noon

> hádegi *(haw-de-ki)*

one o'clock PM

> klukkan er þrettán *(kluch-kan er thre-ht-awn)*

two o'clock PM

> klukkan er fjórtán *(fyohr-tawn)*

midnight

> miðnætti *(midh-nigh-ht-i)*

Icelandic 101: A Practical Guide for Beginners

Duration

_____ **minute(s)**

>_____ mínúta *(meen-oo-ta)*
>
>Plural; mínútur *(meen-oo-tur)*

_____ **hour(s)**

>_____ klukkustund *(kluch-ku-stunt)*
>
>Plural; klukkustundir *(kluch-ku-stunt-ir)*

_____ **day(s)**

>_____ dagur *(dak-ur)*
>
>Plural; dagar *(dak-ar)*

_____ **week(s)**

>_____ vika *(vik-a)*
>
>Plural; vikur *(vik-ur)*

_____ **month(s)**

>_____ mánuður *(maw-nudh-ur)*
>
>Plural; mánuðir *(maw-nudh-ar)*

_____ **year(s)**

>_____ ár *(awr)*

Days

Sunday

    Sunnudagur *(Sun-nu-tak-ur)*

Monday

    Mánudagur *(Maw-nu-tak-ur)*

Tuesday

    Þriðjudagur *(Three-dhyu-tak-ur)*

Wednesday

    Miðvikudagur *(Midh-vee-ku-tak-ur)*

Thursday

    Fimmtudagur *(Fim-tu-tak-ur)*

Friday

    Föstudagur *(Furs-tu-tak-ur)*

Saturday

    Laugardagur *(Lur-ee-kar-tak-ur)*

Icelandic 101: A Practical Guide for Beginners

Months

January

    janúar (yan-oo-ar)

February

    febrúar *(feb-roo-ar)*

March

    mars *(mars)*

April

    apríl *(ap-reel)*

May

    maí (ma-ee) similar to migh in "might"

June

    júní *(yoo-nee)*

July

    júlí *(yoo-lee)*

August

    ágúst *(aw-koo-st)*

September

    september *(sep-tem-ber)*

Phrases & Vocabulary

October

október *(ok-toh-ber)*

November

nóvember *(noh-vem-ber)*

December

desember *(des-em-ber)*

Icelandic 101: A Practical Guide for Beginners

Writing Time and Date

DATE: The date in Iceland is written in the dd/mm/yyyy format, as in Europe.

Example:

> *miðvikudagur 14. apríl 2007*
>
> *Wednesday 14th April 2007*

TIME: The time in Iceland is written in the 24 hour format, as in most of Europe

Examples of time:

> *Written: klukkan 07.05*
>
> *Spoken: "klukkan er fimm mínútur yfir sjö" (kluch-kan er fim meen-oot-ur i-ir syur)*
>
> *Written: klukkan 13.30*
>
> *Spoken: "klukkan er hálftvö" (kluch-kan er hawlv-tvur)*

Sometimes "klukkan" can be shortened to "kl.":

> *Written: kl. 20:45*
>
> *Spoken: "klukkan er korter í níu" (kluch-kan er kor-ter ee neehu)*

Colors

black
>svartur *(svar-tur)*

white
>hvítur *(kvee-tur)*

gray
>grár *(graw-r)*

red
>rauður *(rur-ee-dhur)*

blue
>blár *(blaw-r)*

yellow
>gulur *(gul-ur)*

green
>grænn *(grigh-n)*

orange
>appelsínugulur *(ahp-el-see-nu-gul-ur)*

purple
>fjólublár *(fyo-lu-blaur)*

Icelandic 101: A Practical Guide for Beginners

brown

    brúnn *(broon)*

Transportation

Bus and Train

A single ticket to _____.

> Einn miða, aðra leiðina til _____. *(Ay-dn mi-dha, adh-ra lay-dhin-a til _____.)*

A return ticket to _____.

> Einn miða, báðar leiðir til _____. *(Ay-dn mi-dha, baw-dhar lay-dhin-ir til _____.)*

How much does that cost?

> Hvað kostar það? *(Kvadh kos-tar thadh?)*

Where does this bus/coach go?

> Hvert fer þessi strætó/rúta? *(Kvar fer the-si strigh-toh/roo-ta?)*

Where is the bus/coach to _____?

> Hvar er strætónn/rútan til _____? *(Kvar er strigh-toh/roo-tan til _____?)*

Does this bus stop at _____?

> Stoppar þessi strætó hjá _____? *(Sto-hpar the-si strigh-toh hyaw _____?)*

Does this coach stop in _____?

Icelandic 101: A Practical Guide for Beginners

Stoppar þessi rúta í _____? *(Sto-hpar the-si roo-ta ee _____?)*

When does the bus/coach leave?

Hvenær fer hann/hún? *(Kven-ighr fer han/hoon?)*

When does the bus/coach leave for _____?

Hvenær fer strætónn/rútan til _____? *(Kven-ighr fer strigh-tohn/roo-tan til _____?)*

When does the bus/coach arrive?

Hvenær kemur hann/hún? *(Kven-ighr kem-ur han/hoon?)*

When will the bus/coach arrive in _____?

Hvenær kemur strætónn/rútan í _____? *(Kven-ighr strigh-tohn/roo-tan ee _____?)*

Directions

How do I get to _____?

    Hvernig kemst ég til _____? *(Kver-nik kem-st ye til _____?)*

Where is _____?

    Hvar er _____? *(Kvar er _____?)*

...the bus stop?

    ...strætóstopp? *(...strigh-toh-sto-hp?)*

    Sometimes; ...strætisvagnastopp? *(...strigh-tis-vak-na-sto-hp?)*

...the bus station?

    ...strætóstöðin? *(...strigh-toh-stur-dhin?)*

    Sometimes; ...strætisvagnastöðin? *(...strigh-toh-vak-na-stur-dhin?)*

...the coach station?

    ...biðstöðin? *(...bidh-stur-dhin?)*

    Sometimes; ...stoppistöðin? *(...sto-hpis-stur-dhin?)*

...the airport?

    ...flugvöllurinn? *(...blu-kvojt-lur-inn?)*

...downtown?

Icelandic 101: A Practical Guide for Beginners

...niður í miðbæ? *(ni-dur ee midh-bye)* "bye" like English "Bye"

...the youth hostel?

...farfuglaheimilið? *(...far-fuk-la-hay-mil-idh?)*

...the guest house?

...gistihúsið? *(...gi-sti-hoos-idh?)*

...the British consulate?

...bretsk ræðismannsskrifstofan? *(bre-tsk righ-dhis-mans-skriv-sto-van?)*

Or, the American consulate: ...amerísk ræðimannsskrifstofan?

(am-e-ree-sk righ-dhis-mans-skriv-sto-van?)

Or, the Canadian consulate?: ...kanadísk ræðimannsskrifstofan?

(ka-nad-ee-sk righ-dhis-mans-skriv-sto-van?)

Or, the Australian consulate?: ...ástralsk ræðimannsskrifstofan?

(aw-stral-sk righ-dhis-mans-skriv-sto-van?)

Where are there a lot of...

Hvar er mikið... *(Kvar er mi-kidh...)*

...hotels?

...hótel? *(...hoh-tel?)*

...restaurants?

Phrases & Vocabulary

...veitingahúsin? *(...vay-tin-ka-hoos-in?)*

...bars?

...krár? *(krawr)*

...sites to see?

...ferðamanns ákvörðunarstaðir? *(...fer-dha-mans aw-kvur-dhun-ar-sta-dhir?)*

Can you show me on the map?

Gætiru sýnt mér á kortinu? *(Gai-tiru see-nt m-yer a kort-inu?)*

street

stræti *(strigh-ti)*

turn left

fara til vinstri *(fa-ra til vin-stri)*

turn right

fara til hægri *(fa-ra til high-kri)*

left

vinstri *(vin-stri)*

right

hægri *(high-kri)*

straight ahead

Icelandic 101: A Practical Guide for Beginners

    beint áfram *(bay-nt aw-fram)*

towards the _____

    til _____ *(til)*

past the _____

    framhjá _____ *(fram-hyaw)*

before the _____

    á undan _____ *(aw un-tan)*

opposite (the)

    á móti _____ *(aw moh-ti)*

Watch for the _____.

    leita að _____. *(lay-ta adh)*

intersection

    gatnamót *(gat-nam-oht)*

north

    norður *(nor-dhur)*

south

    suður *(su-dhur)*

east

    austur *(ur-ee-stur)*

Phrases & Vocabulary

west

    vestur *(ve-stur)*

uphill

    upp í móti *(up ee moh-ti)*

downhill

    niður í móti *(ni-dhur ee moh-ti)*

Taxi

Taxi!

> Taxi! *(Tax-ee!)*

Take me to _____, please.

> Taka mig til _____, gjörðu svo vel. *(Ta-ka mik til _____, gyur-dhu svo vel.)*

How much does it cost to get to _____?

> Hvað kostar það til _____? *(Kvadh kos-tar thadh til _____?)*

Take me there, please.

> Taka mig til þar, gjörðu svo vel. *(Ta-ka mik til thar, gyur-dhu svo vel.)*

Lodging

Do you have any rooms available?

Áttu laus herbergi? *(Ow-tu luhys her-ber-ki?)*

I'd like a single/double room.

Gæti ég fengið einsmanns herbergi/tveggjamanna herbergi. *(Gigh-ti ye fen-kidh ay-ns-mans her-ber-ki/tvek-ja-ma-na her-ber-ki.)*

Does the room come with...

Kemur það með... *(Ke-mur thadh medh...)*

...bedsheets?

...rúmföt? *(...room-furt?)*

...a bathroom?

...klósett? *(...kloh-se-ht?)*

...a telephone?

...sími? *(...see-mi?)*

...a TV?

...sjónvarp? *(...syohn-varp?)*

...a bath/shower?

...baði/sturtu? *(...ba-dhi/stuhr-tu?)*

Icelandic 101: A Practical Guide for Beginners

May I see the room first?

> Má ég sjá herbergið fyrst? *(Maw ye syaw her-berg-ith fi-rst?)*

Do you have anything quieter?

> Ertu nokkuð með ró herbergi? *(Er-tu no-chk-udh medh roh her-ber-ki?)*

...bigger?

> ...stórt herbergi? *(...stoh-rt her-ber-ki?)*

...cleaner?

> ...hreinna herbergi? *(...hraydna her-ber-ki?)*

...cheaper?

> ...ódýrara herbergi? *(...oh-deer-a-ra her-ber-ki)*

OK, I'll take it.

> Allt í lagi, ég tek það.

I will stay for _____ night(s).

> Ég dvelst hér _____ nótt/nætur.

Can you suggest another hotel?

> Hefur þú annað hótel að áforma?

Do you have a safe?

> Hefur þú öryggishólfi?

...lockers?

...hirslur?

Is breakfast/supper included?

Er morgunmatur/kvöldmatur innifalinn?

What time is breakfast/supper?

Hvenær er morgunmaturinn/kvöldmaturinn?

Please clean my room.

Getur þú hreinsa herbergi mitt?

Can you wake me at _____?

Getur þú vekja mig klokkan _____?

I want to check out.

Get ég skrá sig út núna?.

Money

How much does it/that cost?

>Hvað kostar það?

Where's the bank?

>Hvar er bankinn?

Do you accept American/Australian/Canadian dollars?

>Þiggur þú Amerískar/Ástralskar/Kanadískar dollara?

Do you accept British pounds?

>Þiggur þú bresk pund?

Do you accept credit cards?

>Þiggur þú greiðslukort?

Can you change money for me?

>Getur þú hjálpað mig að breyta peninga?

Where can I get money changed?

>Hvar get ég fengið breyt peninga?

Can you change a traveler's cheque for me?

>Getur þú breytt ferðatékka fyrir mig?

Where can I get a traveler's cheque changed?

    Hvar get ég fengið ferðastávísanir?

What is the exchange rate for?

    Hvað er skiptið fyrir___?

Where is an automatic teller machine (ATM)?

    Hvar er nálægastur skammtari?

Eating

A table for one person/two people, please.

    Get ég fengið borð fyrir eitt persónu/tvö fólk.

Can I look at the menu, please?

    Get ég sjéð matseðil?

Is there a house specialty?

    Hvað er sérstakur ykkar?

Is there a local specialty?

    Er það staðarréttur ég á bergja?

I'm a vegetarian.

    Ég er grænmetisæta.

I don't eat pork.

    Ég borða ekki svínakjöt.

I don't eat beef.

    Ég borða ekki nautakjöt.

I only eat kosher food.

    Ég borða aðeins réttfæðu.

breakfast

    morgunkaffi This translates as *morning coffee* .

lunch

>hádegisverður

tea (*meal*)

>síðdegistur

supper

>kvöldmatur

I would like _____.

>Get ég haft _____?.

I want a dish containing _____.

>Ég vil hafa rétt með _____.

chicken

>kjúklingi

beef

>nautakjöti

fish

>fiski.

meat

>kjöti

ham

Icelandic 101: A Practical Guide for Beginners

    svínslæri

sausages

    pylsum

cheese

    osti

eggs

    eggjum

salad

    salati

(fresh) vegetables

    (ferskar) grænmeti

(fresh) fruit

    (ferskar) ávöxtur

bread

    brauð

toast

    smurt brauð

noodles

    núðlur

rice

> rhrísgrjón

beans

> baunir

May I have a glass of _____?

> Get ég fengið glas _____?

May I have a cup of _____?

> Get ég fengið bolla _____?

May I have a bottle of _____?

> Get ég fengið flösku _____?

coffee

> kaffi

milk

> mjólk (noun) mjólka (verb)

tea (*drink*)

> te

juice

> safi

(bubbly) water

Icelandic 101: A Practical Guide for Beginners

> karbónatvatn

water

> vatn

beer

> bjór

red/white wine

> rauð/hvítvín

May I have some _____?

> Get ég fengið hluti _____?

salt

> salt.

black pepper

> svartur pipar

butter

> smjör

chocolate

> súkkulaði

Excuse me, waiter? *(getting attention of server)*

> Afsakið, þjónn?

I'm finished.

> Ég hef klárað.

The meal was delicious.

> Máltíðir var yndislegur.

Please clear the plates.

> Getur þú tekið með diski?

The check, please.

> Get ég fengið reikningi?

Icelandic 101: A Practical Guide for Beginners

Bars

Do you serve alcohol?

>Þjónið þið vínandi?

Is there table service?

>Komið þið til borðs?

A beer/two beers, please.

>Get ég fengið bjór/tvo bjórar?.

A glass of red/white wine, please.

>Get ég fengið gler rauð/hvítvín?.

A pint, please.

>Get ég fengið hálfpottur?.

In a bottle, please.

>Get ég fengið það í flösku?.

_____ (*hard liquor*) and _____ (*mixer*), please.

>Get ég fengið_____ og _____?.

whiskey

>viskí

vodka

>vodka

Phrases & Vocabulary

rum

    romm

water

    vatn

club soda

    club soda

tonic

    hressing

orange juice

    appelsína safi

Coke (*soda*)

    Coka-Cola

Do you have any bar snacks?

    Hafið þið barskyndibita?

One more, please.

    Get ég fengið annar?.

Another round, please.

    Annar hringur!

When is closing time?

Icelandic 101: A Practical Guide for Beginners

> Hvenær lokið þið?

Cheers!

> Skál!

Shopping

Do you have this in my size?

>Hefur þú þessi í stærð minn?

How much is this?

>Hvað kostar það?

That's too expensive.

>Hinn er of dýr.

expensive

>dýr

cheap

>ódýr

I can't afford it.

>Ég get haft efni á því.

I don't want it.

>Ég vil það ekki.

I'm not interested.

>Ég hef áhuga á því ekki. (..)

OK, I'll take it.

>Allt í lagi, ég tek það.

Icelandic 101: A Practical Guide for Beginners

Can I have a bag?

    Get ég fengið poka?

Do you ship (overseas)?

    Getur þú senda málefni til ___?

I need...

    Mig langar...

...toothpaste.

    ...tannkrem.

...a toothbrush.

    ...tannbursta.

...tampons.

    ...vattrúllur.

...soap.

    ...sápu.

...shampoo.

    ...hárþvott.

...pain reliever.(e.g., aspirin or ibuprofen)

    ...verkjalyf.

Phrases & Vocabulary

...cold medicine.

 ...læknisfræði fyrir kvef.

...stomach medicine.

 ...magalæknisfræði.

...a razor.

 ...rakvél.

...an umbrella.

 ...regnhlíf.

...sunblock lotion.

 ...sólhúðkrem.

...a postcard.

 ...póstkort.

...postage stamps.

 ...frímerki.

...batteries.

 ...rafhlöður.

...writing paper.

 ...skrifapappír.

...a pen.

Icelandic 101: A Practical Guide for Beginners

...penna.

...English-language books.

...bækur á ensku.

...English-language magazines.

...tímarit á ensku.

...an English-language newspaper.

...dagblað á ensku.

...an English-Icelandic dictionary.

...ensk-íslensk orðabók.

Driving

I want to rent a car.

> Get ég leigt bíl?

Can I get insurance?

> Get ég fengið vátryggingu?

stop *(on a street sign)*

> stans

one way

> einstefna

yield

> biðskylda

no parking

> engin bílastæði

speed limit

> hraðatak

gas (*petrol* **) station**

> bensínstöð

garage

> verkstæði

Icelandic 101: A Practical Guide for Beginners

petrol

    bensín

diesel

    díselknúinn

Phrases & Vocabulary

Authority.

I haven't done anything wrong.

> Ég hef ekki gert nokkuð rangt.

It was a misunderstanding.

> Það var misskilningur.

Where are you taking me?

> Hvert eruð þið að taka mig?

Am I under arrest?

> Er ég handtekin(n)?

I am an American/Australian/British/Canadian citizen.

> Ég er Amerískur/Breskur/Ástralskur borgari.

I demand to talk to the American/Australian/British/Canadian embassy/consulate.

> Ég krafa tala með Amerískri/Ástralskri/Breskri sendiráðinu/ræðismannsskrifstofunni.

I want to talk to a lawyer.

> Ég vil tala við lögfræðing.

Can I just pay a fine now?

Icelandic 101: A Practical Guide for Beginners

Má ég bara borgað sekt núna?

Bonus Icelandic Slang

Deita: to date

Gemsi: cell/mobile phone

Kúl: cool

Skinka: a woman obsessed with tanning

Ógeðslega: very

Geðveikt: very

Geðveikt: crazy (good and bad)

Dissa: to bother someone intentionally

Djúsa: to drink alcohol

Snilld: brilliance

Made in the USA
Middletown, DE
13 July 2020